Decodable Readers

Take-Home Blackline Masters

HOUGHTON MIFFLIN   BOSTON

Roz the Vet

by Terry Rengifo

illustrated by Joe Cepeda

Roz the vet can help a pet!
Roz can zip in a red van.

1

Roz can look at a pet pig.
Roz fed it. Gob, gob, gob.

2

22F

Tab can look at Roz.
Roz will get Tab down.

Roz the vet can help a pet!
Roz can zip in a red van.

6

3

23F

Vic had a bad cut.
Can Roz fix it? Roz can!

Tab Cat got out. Tab ran.
Tab had fun. Tab ran up.

4

5

24F

Not Yet

by Nancy Spencer

Cat, do not get up yet!
Nap on the red cat mat.

1

Dog, do not get up yet!
Nap on the big rug.

2

Bat, get up! Bat, take off!
Bats can quit at sun up!

Hen, do not get up yet!
Nap in the hen box.

6

3

Pig, do not get up yet!
Nap in the pig pen.

4

Fox, do not get up yet!
Nap in the fox den.

5

Can Not Quit Yet

by Antonio Winkler

illustrated by Rick Brown

Yes, yes! Ben can hit it.

Ben hit the tub, rum tum!

1

Rum! Tum! Tum!

Ben can not quit yet.

2

It can zip, zip, zip.

Meg can not quit yet.

Yes, yes! Kim can dig.

Kim can dig, dig, dig.

6

3

31F

Kim can dig, dig, dig.
Kim can not quit yet.

Yes, yes! It can take off.
Zip, zip, Meg! Zip, zip!

4

5

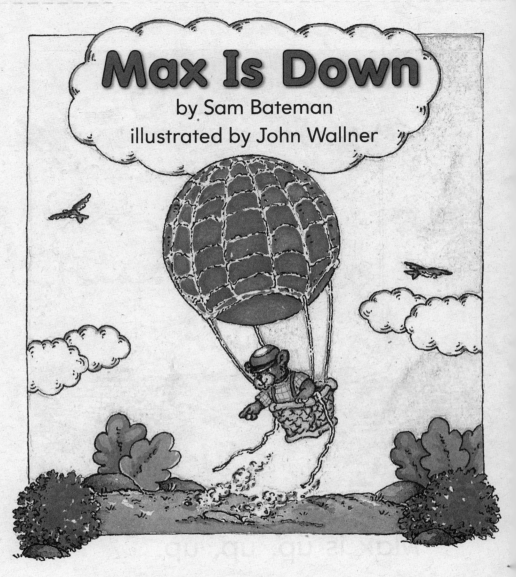

Max Is Down

by Sam Bateman

illustrated by John Wallner

Max can go up, up, up.

Max will go up, up, up.

1

Max is up, up, up.

Max can not get down.

"Help!" said Max.

2

Yes. He did!

Big Zeb got Max down.

6

Bud ran.

Can Bud get Max down?

Look! Bud can not get Max.

3

35F

Tom ran. Can Tom get Max?

Look! Tom can not get Max.

Big Zeb can help us.

4

Big Zeb can tug, tug, tug.

Will Max get down?

Tug, Big Zeb, tug!

Will Max get down?

5

A Fun Job

by Priscilla Banab

illustrated by Jeff Mack

Ted has a job.

Deb has a job.

1

"Find nuts," said Mom.

"Get nuts. Get lots."

Ted runs. Deb runs.

2

38F

Ted hid nuts in pots.
Deb hid nuts in pots.
What is in the pots now?

Ted got nuts. Deb got nuts.
It is a fun job to get nuts.
It is fun, fun, fun.

6

3

39F

Ted hid nuts.

Ted hid nuts in pots.

Deb hid nuts in pots.

Look at the pots.

Can Ted and Deb see nuts?

No, Ted and Deb can not.

4

5

40F

See What We Can Do

by Susan Gorman-Howe

illustrated by Sue Dennen

4

1

1A

2

3

2A

We Can Make It

by Susan Gorman-Howe

illustrated by Anthony Lewis

4

1

3A

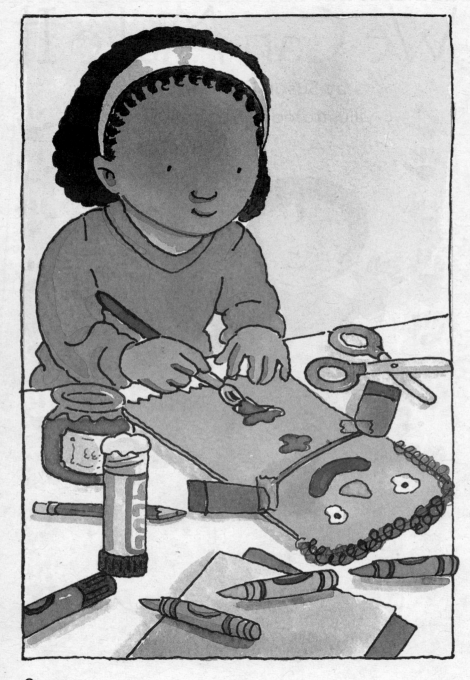

2

3

4A

We Go to School

by Susan Gorman-Howe

illustrated by Maryann Cocca-Leffler

4

1

5A

Welcome to Kindergarten

2

3

I Like

by Owen Marcus

illustrated by Maribel Suarez

I like .

I like .

4

4 1

7A

I like .

I like .

2

3

8A

Baby Bear's Family

by Susan Gorman-Howe

illustrated by Angela Jarecki

4

1

2

3

10A

The Party

by Ron Kingsley

illustrated by Yvette Banek

I like the .

I like the .

4

1

11A

I like the .

2

I like the .

3

Mm

Mm

by Pat Macnan

illustrated by
Diana Schoenbrun

4

1

13A

Mm

M m

2

3

14A

Mm

I like the  and the 🧁🧁.

4

Unit 1/Week 4/Selection 2

I Like Mm
by Pat Macnan

I like the 🌙.

1

I like the  .

I like the .

2

3

16A

Ss

by Pat Macnan

illustrated by Diana Schoenbrun

4

1

Ss

Ss

2

3

18A

S s

I like the and the ⬙.

4

I Like Ss
by Pablo Lopez

I like the ⛵.

1

Ss

I like the .

2

Ss

I like the ☀.

3

20A

Unit 2
Show and Tell

Contents

Aa

Aa

by Roberto Livingston

illustrated by Bernard Adnet

4

1

Aa

Aa

2

3

2B

Aa

I see the .

4

3B

I See

by Sheila Hoffman

I see the .

1

Aa

I see the .

2

Aa

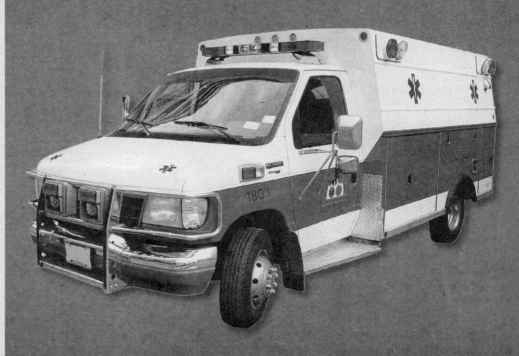

I see the .

3

T t

T t

by Nimesh Sing

illustrated by Priscilla Burris

T t

6B

T t

Tt

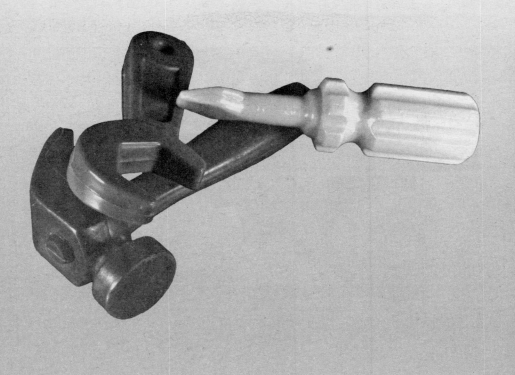

We like the 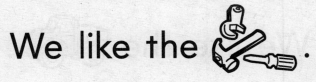.

4

We Like Toys

by Matthew Lorer

1

Tt

Tt

We like the .

We like the .

2

3

8B

Cc

9B

Cc

by David Ashford

illustrated by John Segal

Cc

Cc

2

3

10B

Cc

I see a  .

4

I Can See

by Laticia Craven

I see a  .

1

Cc

Cc

I see a .

I see a .

P p

4

P p

by Diondra Thomas
illustrated by Kristin Sorra

1

Pp

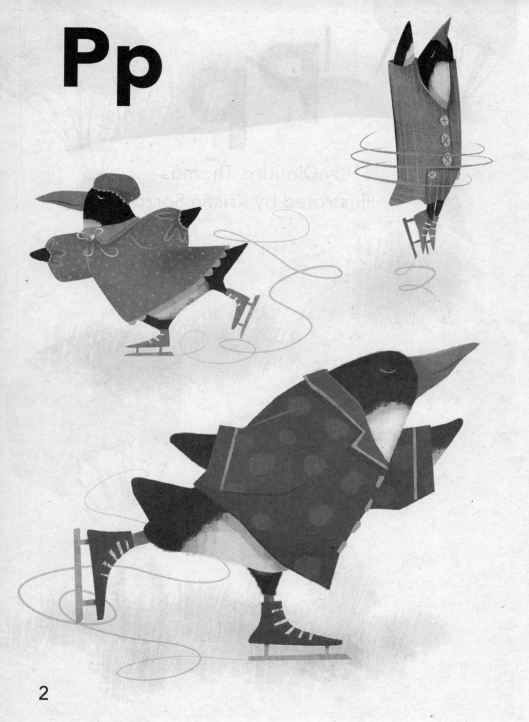

Pp

2

3

14B

Pp

I like to see .

4

I Like Animals

by Sydney Mueller

I like to see .

1

Pp

I like to see .

2

Pp

I like to see 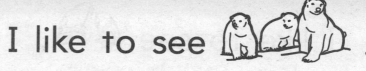.

3

We like to see  .

4

Mmmm, Good!

by Angela Ferie

illustrated by Ana Ochoa

I see .

1

I like .

2

We like .

3

We like the .

The Playground

by Paul Falcon

illustrated by Robin Oz

I like the .

4

1

I like to .

We see the .

2

3

Unit 3
Outside My Door

Contents

Come and See Me

by Greg Kent

Come to me.

Come to me, Sam.

Sam Cat sat.

Mac Cat, Mac Cat!

Mac, Mac, Mac!

4

1

1C

Come to me, Mac Cat.
Mac Cat sat.

Sam Cat, Sam Cat!
Sam, Sam, Sam!

2

3

2C

I pat Pam.

Pat, pat, pat.

4

Pam and Me

by Louise Andreas

illustrated by Judith Lanfredi

Pam, Pam, Pam, Pam!

1

Pam, Pam, Pam.
Come to me, Pam.

2

I sat. Pam Cat sat.

3

I Can Nap

by Christopher Lawrence

I can nap with my 🧸 .
Nap, nap, nap, nap.

🐻 can nap.
Nap, nap, nap, nap.

4

1

5C

I can nap with my .

Nap, nap, nap, nap.

2

 can nap.

Nap, nap, nap, nap.

3

Tap with Me

by Cara Blanco

illustrated by Holli Conger

I am Tap Man!

Tap, tap, tap! Tap Man!

4

I can tap.

I tap, tap, tap.

1

7C

I can tap. Nan can tap.
Nan can tap, tap, tap.

2

8C

I can tap with Nan.
Tap, Nan. Tap.

3

What Can You See?

by Leyla Rogers

illustrated by Shari Halpern

Can Mac see you?

Cam can see a tan cat.

A tan, tan, tan cat!

Cam can see a fat tan cat.

4

1

9C

Fan can see Jac.

Can Jac see Fan?

Jac can! Jac can!

Sam can see Nat nap.

Nap, nap, nap, Nat!

2

3

Can you see the fat cat?
What a fat, fat, fat cat!

4

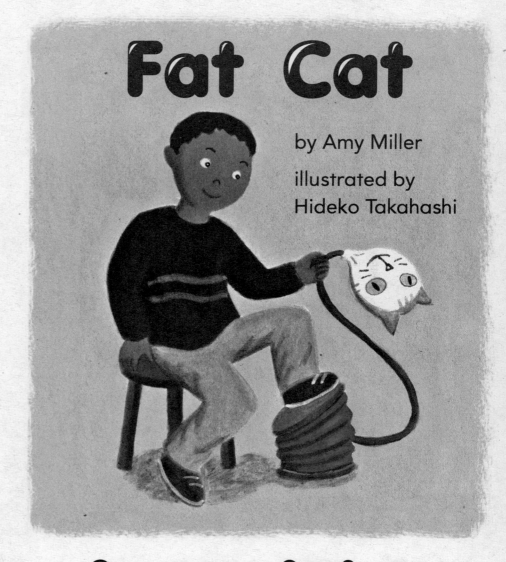

Fat Cat

by Amy Miller

illustrated by
Hideko Takahashi

Can you see Sam?
Sam can tap, tap, tap.

1

Tap, Sam, tap.
Tap, tap, tap, Sam.

Tap, Sam!
Tap. Tap. Tap.

2

3

12C

Now we can nap, nap, nap.

4

13C

What Now?
by Suzanne Gerardi

Can Pam and Nan pat?

Nan can pat now.

1

Can Fab tap? Fab can!
Fab can tap now.

2

Sam and Bab are at bat.
Bat, Sam, bat!

3

14C

Pat! Pat! Pat! Pat!
We are 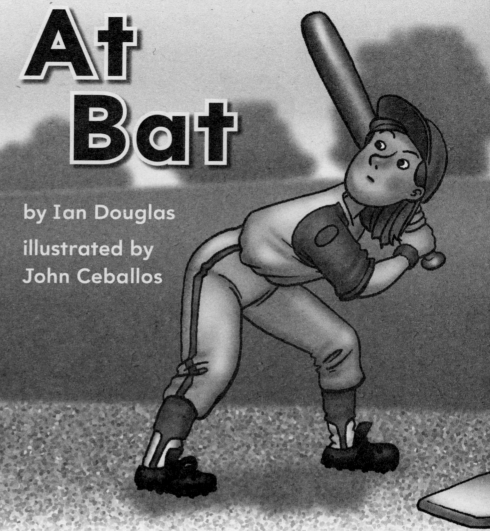, Pat!

4

At Bat

by Ian Douglas

illustrated by
John Ceballos

See Bab at bat.
Bab can bat, bat, bat.

1

Bat now, Bab!
Bam!

See Pat.
Pat. Pat! Pat!

2

3

Pam Cat

by Nina Dimopolous

illustrated by Bari Weissmann

Mac sat and sat.

1

Pam, Pam, Pam!

Come to me Pam Cat.

4

Pam Cat sat.

Mac can pat Pam Cat.

2

Pam Cat sat, sat, sat.

Mac can fan Pam Cat.

3

18C

Nat sat. Bab sat. Nan sat.

4

Come with Me

by Roger DiPaulo

illustrated by Fahimeh Amiri

Nat sat and sat.

Nat sat, sat, sat.

1

Come with me, Bab!
Bab! Bab! Bab!

Nat sat. Bab sat.
Nat can see Nan.
Bab can see Nan.

2

3

Unit 4
Let's Find Out

Contents

What Is It?
by Orlando Sosa

Tam can pin it. Pin, pin, pin.

What is it, Tam?

1

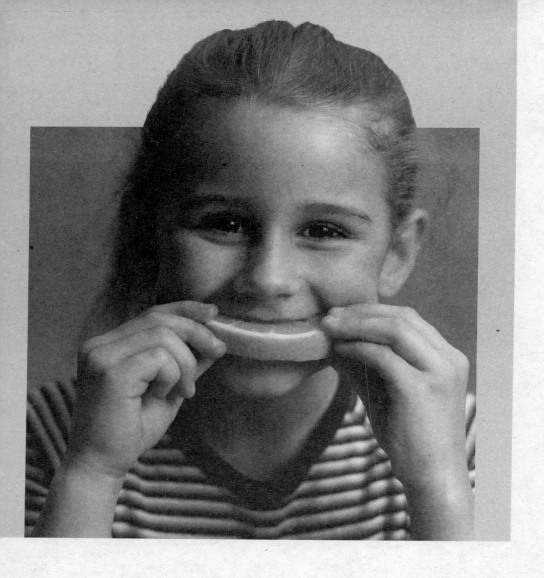

Tif bit it. Bit, bit, bit.
What is it, Tif?

2

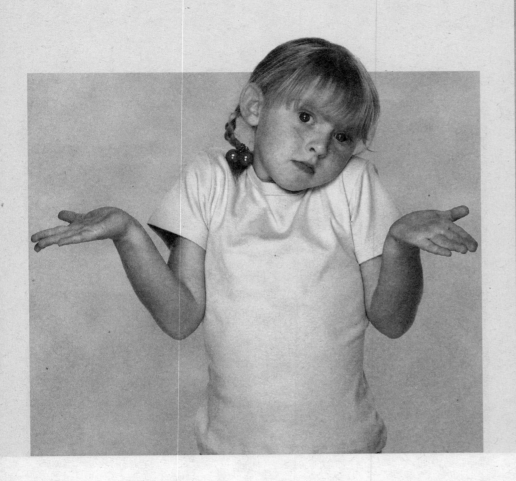

Pam can see it.
What is it, Pam?

Mac can nip it. Nip, nip, nip.
What is it, Mac?

6

3

3D

It can fit Cam. Fit, fit, fit.
What is it, Cam?

Tim can pat it. Pat, pat, pat.
What is it, Tim?

4

5

4D

It Is My Cab

by Amy Miller-Krezelak
illustrated by Joe Boddy

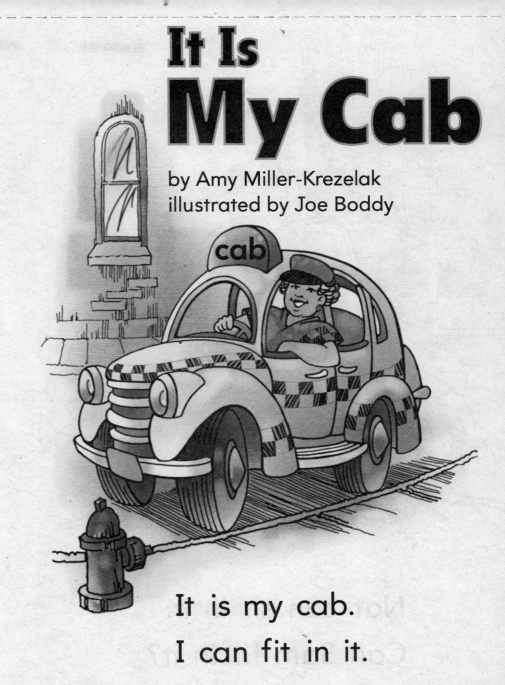

It is my cab.
I can fit in it.

1

Nat can sit in it.
Can Sam fit in it?

2

See, we can fit.
It is OK!

Sam can fit. Can Mac fit?
Mac can fit. Sit, sit, sit!

6

3

7D

Can Bab fit?

Bab can fit. Sit, sit, sit!

Nat, Sam, Bab, Mac fit.

Now how can I fit in it?

Can You Find It?

by Randi Livingston

Min can fit in this.

Min can sit in it. Find Min.

1

Tim can fit in this.
Tim can sit in it. Find Tim.

2

Can Nan find Tam?
Nan can! Nan can!

6

Gab can sit in this.
Gab can fit in it.

3

11D

Gig can sit in this cap.
Find Gig in it.

Tig is in this bag.
Find Tig in it.

4

5

12D

Gig Pig

by Zev Herschel

illustrated by Liz Callen

This pig is Gig Pig.
Can Gig Pig find Pat Cat?

1

This is Pat Cat.

Can Pat Cat find Gig Pig?

2

14D

Pat Cat can sit with Gig Pig.
Bim bam, bim bam!

6

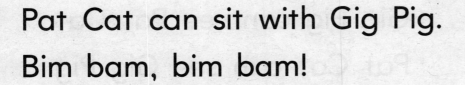

Bim bam, bim bam!
Bim bam, bim!

3

15D

Tac, tac, tac, tac!
Tac, tac, tac!

4

Gig Pig can see Pat Cat.
Pat Cat can see Gig Pig.

5

What Will It Be?

by Daniel Osterman

Tab! Tab! Tab! Tab!

Will Tab be big, big, big?

1

Tab will be big.

Big Tab can nap, nap, nap.

2

18D

Rab will be big.
Big Rab can sit, sit, sit.

Ric! Ric! Ric! Ric!
Will Ric be big, big, big?

6

3

19D

Ric will be big.
Big Ric can sip, sip, sip.

Rab! Rab! Rab! Rab!
Will Rab be big, big, big?

4

5

Rac Is It

by Wendy Sinclair

illustrated by Diane Blasius

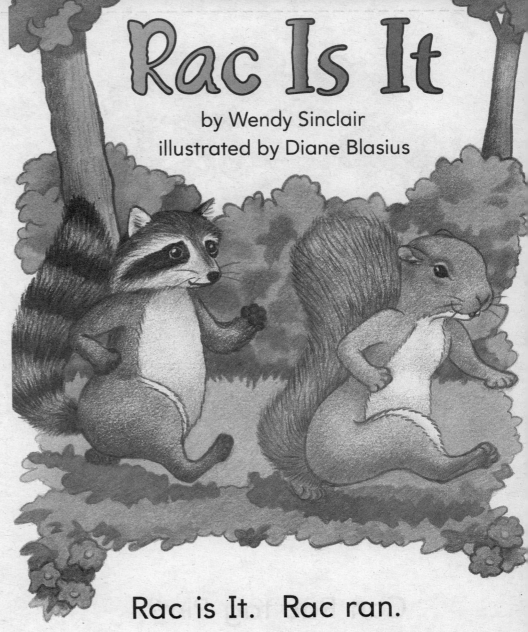

Rac is It. Rac ran.

Pim ran, ran, ran.

1

Can Rac tag Pim?

Rac can tag Pim.

2

22D

Can Rac tag Pim now?

Pim will be It now.

Can Pim tag Rac?

6

3

23D

Rac is It.

Can Rac tag Pim?

Pim ran, ran, ran.

Unit 4/Week 3/Selection 2

Go for It!

by William Alfred

illustrated by Jill Dubin

Tif can dig.

Go for it, Tif! Dig, dig, dig.

1

Nan can dab.

Go for it, Nan!

Dab, dab, dab, dab.

2

26D

Tad and Pam can dip.

Go for it! Dip, dip, dip.

6

Mim can sip.

Go for it, Mim!

Sip, sip, sip.

3

Dan can tap the sap.

Go for it, Dan! Tap, tap, tap.

Sid can pat the big pig.

Go for it, Sid! Pat, pat, pat.

4

5

28D

D Is for Dad

by David McCoy

illustrated by Lisa Thiesing

D is for Dad.

Dad, dad, dad, dad, dad.

1

D is for dig.
Dig, dig, dig, dig, dig.

2

D is for dad. Dad, dad, dad.

Dad Pig is my dad!

Dad Pig can sit in a rig.

Dad Pig can dig, dig, dig.

6

3

31D

Dad Pig can be at bat.
Bat it, Dad. Bat it.

Dad Pig can go in for a dip.
Go for it, Dad!

4

5

32D

The Big Dig

by David Michaels

illustrated by Robin Koontz

Bab will dig, dig, dig.
Bab will go find Sid.

1

Bab can rap, rap, rap.

Bab can tap, tap, tap.

2

34D

Bab can pat.

Sid can pat.

Tim can pat.

It is big, big, big!

Sid is in.

Bab did find Sid.

6

3

35D

Bab can dig.

Sid can dig with Bab.

Bab and Sid dig, dig, dig.

Tim can dig with Bab.

Tim can dig with Sid.

Tim, Bab, and Sid can dig.

4

5

We Fit

by Cindy Evans

illustrated by Tim Bowers

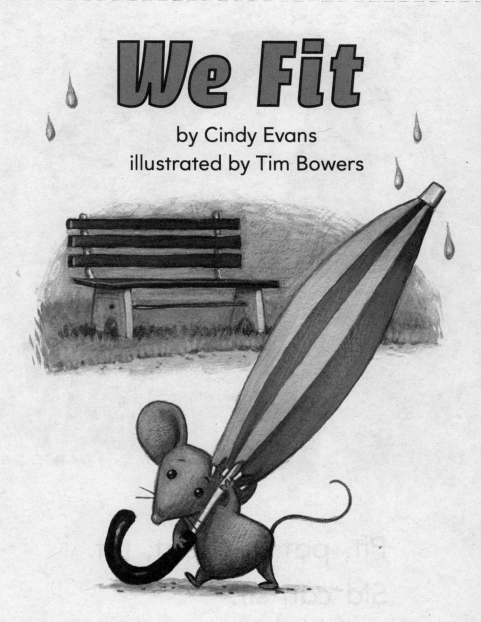

Pit, pat, pit, pat, pit, pat.

1

37D

Pit, pat, pit, pat, pit.

Sid can sit.

Sid can fit.

2

This is how Tim will fit.

Tim, Mac, Rib, and Sid sit.

Pit, pat, pit, pat, pit.

6

Pit, pat, pit, pat, pit.

Can Mac fit?

Can Mac sit with Sid?

3

Pit, pat, pit, pat, pit.

Can Rib fit?

Will Rib, Mac, and Sid sit?

4

Pit, pat, pit, pat, pit.

Sid can fit. Mac can fit.

Rib can fit.

How will Tim fit?

5

Unit 5
Growing and Changing

Contents

Make It Pop!

by Kari Matheson

Mim can make it big.
It will pop.

1

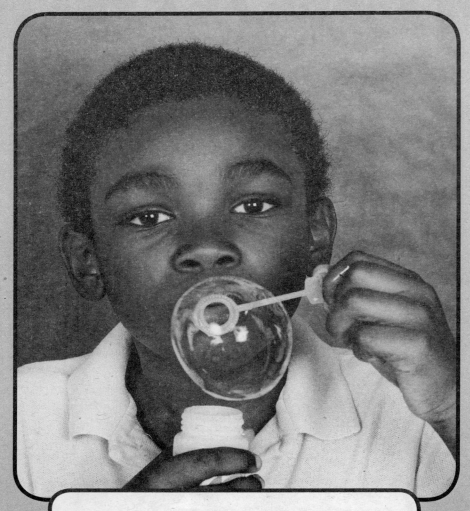

Tom can make it big.
It will pop.

2

Rob can make it big.
Will it pop?

6

Dot and Pat play.
Pop it, Dot! Pop it, Pat!

3

3E

Cam can make it pop.
Pop it, Cam! Pop it! Pop it!

4

Con can make it pop!
Pop it, Con! Pop it! Pop it!

5

4E

My Dog Tom

by Amy Miller-Krezelak

illustrated by Amanda Harvey

Tom is my dog.

Tom can sit with me.

1

Tom can nap on this pad.

The pad Tom naps on is tan.

2

Tom got big!

Tom and I got big.

Tom can play.

Tom can nip, nip, nip!

6

3

7E

Tom can dig a big pit.

Tom can dig, dig, dig!

Can Tom play tag?

4

Tom can play tag.

I can tag Tom.

Tom can tag me.

5

8E

A Good Job

by Spiro Dantous

Rod got a job in a rig.
Rod can sit in the rig.

1

"I got a job," said Jon.

Jon can dig, dig, dig, dig!

2

10E

Mac Dog got a good job.
Jan can not see. Mac can.

Dom got a job in a cab.
Dom can sit in the cab.

6

3

Dot got a job. Dot can tap.
Dot can tap, tap, tap.

Jin can make jam, jam, jam!
"I got a good job," said Jin.

4

5

12E

Fix It!

by Sue Chang
illustrated by John Berg

The map got a rip in it.
"Ox did it," said Fox.
"Ox did it."

1

"A job for Ox!," said Dog.

"Fix it! Fix it, Ox. Fix it!"

2

"I can fix it, Ox." Dog did.
Dog did fix it. Good job, Dog!

The cap got a rip in it.
"Fox! Fox did it," said Ox.

6

3

15E

"Fox can fix it," said Dog.
"Fix it, fix it, fix it, Fox!"

The box got a big rip in it.
"I did it. I did it," said Dog.

4

5

16E

My Pet Dog

by Nina Walker

All ten pets can fit.

All ten pets can sit.

1

Ben is a pet dog.

Can Ben get a pat?

2

18E

Peg can fit in the bag.
Peg can sit in it.

Ted is a pet dog.
Can Ted get a pat?

6

3

19E

Deb ran, ran, ran.
What did she get?

Meg ran, ran, ran.
What did she get?

4

5

20E

Ben and Jen

by Debbie Dixon

illustrated by Susan Calitri

"Jen, Jen, Jen!" said Ben.

"I can not get Jen."

1

"Get a net," said Ed.

Ben can not get Jen.

2

22E

"I can get Jen," said Meg.
Meg did get Jen.

"Get a box," said Ted.
Ben can not get Jen.

6

3

Can Meg get Jen?

She can not get Jen.

Ed and Ted got men.

Ben and Meg got men.

Hog in a Hat

by David McCoy

illustrated by Elizabeth Sayles

Hog can sit.

He can sit in a big top hat.

1

Dog can sit.

She can sit in a red hat.

2

Pig can nap.

She can nap in a red hat.

Cat can sit.

He can sit in a tan hat.

6

3

Hen ran.

She ran in a red hat.

Fox can hop.

He can hop in a big hip hat.

4

5

28E

Kid Hid

by David McCoy

illustrated by Steven Parton

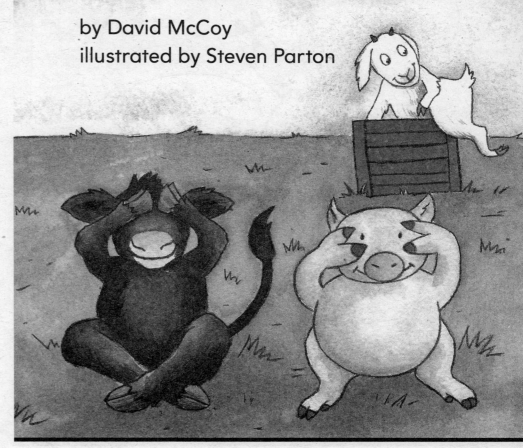

Kid hid.

Can he fit in a red box?

1

No, Kid can not fit in it.

Kim can find him.

2

Kim can not find him!

Kip can not find him!

Kid hid.

Can he fit in a jet kit?

6

3

31E

No, Kid can not fit in it.

Kip can find him.

Kid hid.

Can he fit in a big pot?

4

5

32E

Six Pigs Hop

by Diana Sheaffer

illustrated Kate Flanagan

Six pigs sit in a pen.

"Sit good pigs, sit," said Jen.

1

Six pigs hop in the pen.

Hop, pigs, hop, hop, hop.

2

34E

Six pigs can sit.

Six pigs can dig in the pen.

"Dig pigs, dig," said Jen.

6

All six pigs hop, hop, hop!

Hop, hop, hop!

3

Six pigs go for a dip.

Dip pigs. Dip pigs. Dip, dip.

Can pigs play?

Six pigs can play.

Six pigs can see Jen.

She can see six pigs.

4

5

Play Kid, Play

by Franco Denehy

illustrated by Sarah Snow

Dad Fox had a big box.

Dad Fox hid it.

1

Dad Fox hid the big box.

Can Red Hen find it?

Red Hen did find it.

2

38E

Kid Fox gets the big box. It had a sax. She can play it.

"It is not for me," said Red Hen. "It is not. It is not."

6

3

Can Jon Dog find the big box Dad Fox hid? Jon Dog did find it.

"It is not for me," said Jon Dog. "Kid Fox! Kid Fox! Dad Fox hid this box!"

4

5

40E

Unit 6
Look at Us

Contents

All In

by Bonnie Whitmark

Can you see Kit?
Kit has fun in a bag.

1

Do you see pups?

Pups can tug, tug, tug, tug.

2

This big cat can run.

It can go up, up, up.

Pups can run down.

Pups can run, run, run, run.

6

3F

3

Big dogs can dig.
Big dogs dug, dug, dug, dug.

Big dogs can run down.
Big dogs can run, run, run.

4

5

4F

Bug and Cat

by James Parsons

illustrated by John Hovell

Bug and Cat can play.

Fun, fun, fun, fun!

1

Bug can hop up and down.

Up, up, up. Fun, fun, fun!

2

Do Bug and Cat run?
Bug and Cat run, run, run!

Cat can hit this for fun.
Rum, tum, tum! Rum, tum!

6

3

7F

Bug can hum. Cat can hum.

Hum, Bug. Hum, Cat.

4

Bug can sit on a rug.

Cat can sit on a rug.

5

Win a Cup!

by Todd Turriro

illustrated by Marilyn Janovitz

Meg can run, run, run!
Meg can win a big cup.

1

Ken can hit and run.

Ken can win a big cup.

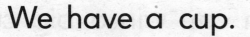

We have a cup.

Pam can hit ten down.

Pam can win a big cup.

6

3

11F

Wes can help Lon.
Lon can help Wes.

Wes can win a big cup!
Lon can win a big cup!

4

5

12F

Wes Can Help

by Anne Miranda

illustrated by Susan Lexa

Len and Lin get on a big jet.

Len and Lin can have fun.

1

Wes led Len. Len can sit.

Wes led Lin. Lin can sit.

2

14F

Len had fun. Lin had fun.
Wes had fun.

6

Len let Wes help him.
Wes got the big bag up.

3

Wes got Len a hot dog.

Wes got Lin a sub.

4

The big jet is down.

Len can run. Lin can run.

5

16F

Vet on a Job!

by Anne Miranda

Ed the vet can look at Max.

1

Sal the vet can look at Viv.
Sal fed the cub.

2